GLOBAL GOURMET

To Elaine,

COOK UP SOME FUN!

2012

GLOBAL GOURMET

A MULTICULTURAL COOKBOOK

Written and Illustrated By Kathleen Bart

Reverie
PUBLISHING COMPANY

This book is dedicated to the joy of creating, sharing and enjoying good food with family, friends and neighbors throughout the world.

A special thank you to my brother Robert, a fellow gourmet, for his encouragement and for sharing his expertise and enthusiasm for fine food.

First edition / Second printing

To purchase additional copies of this book, please contact:
Reverie Publishing Company
130 South Wineow Street
Cumberland, MD 21502
888-721-4999
www.reveriepublishing.com

Library of Congress Control Number 2003094471
ISBN: 978-1-932485-09-7

Design: Anna Christian
Production Assistant: Anna Goddu

Printed and bound in Korea

BEFORE YOU GET COOKING...
SOME IMPORTANT REMINDERS!

Global Gourmet is designed to delight, educate and entertain aspiring chefs of all ages! Please take a few minutes to read the following reminders before you begin cooking, to ensure that your experience in the kitchen is a safe and satisfying one.

A special note to young chefs and their families: Young chefs should always cook with the assistance and supervision of an adult. Many recipes in this book require the use of a hot oven and burners, electrical appliances and sharp tools. Prevent accidents by handling these with caution, and with the help of an adult. The author and publisher cannot accept responsibility for any accidents that may occur while preparing the recipes in this book. Please be responsible for your own safety in the kitchen!

It's also a good idea to read every recipe all the way through before you begin to cook, to make sure you have all the equipment required, as well as enough time, to prepare it.

Your global journey is about to begin!

Global Gourmet is your passport to the cuisines and cultures of the world. Choose a destination, select a menu and cook up a recipe to learn how people around the globe celebrate food, life and culture!

Bon Voyage!

CONTENTS

AFRICA

MENU

SUNSET SUPPER ON THE AFRICAN SAVANNAH

Lemon Squash

Groundnut Stew

Rice Balls

Sautéed Spinach

Coconut Ice Cream

Lemon Squash

INGREDIENTS *(serves 4)*

4 cups water
1 cup superfine sugar
6 large lemons

DIRECTIONS

1 Roll the lemons back and forth on a counter top for a minute or two. This motion will loosen the juice from the lemons.

2 Cut 5 of the lemons in half. Squeeze the lemons, collecting the juice in a medium-sized bowl. When all 5 lemons have been squeezed, pour the juice through a fine strainer into a large pitcher.

3 Add the superfine sugar to the lemon juice in the pitcher, stirring until dissolved.

4 Stir in the water. Cut the remaining lemon into thin slices and add to the pitcher. Refrigerate several hours.

5 Serve in glasses over crushed or cubed ice.

African Lemonade

Lemon Squash is the African interpretation of lemonade. This beverage is rather descriptively named "squash" because the lemons must be squashed and squeezed to render their tart juice. Squash does not have to be limited to lemon varieties. Oranges and limes work just as well with this recipe.

African Textile Designs

The individuals illustrated on the facing page are wearing clothing created with African textile designs. The woman on the far left wears a wrap garment, which has been tie-dyed, creating a circular motif. The woman on the right wears an indigo Batik. A Batik is created by painting wax designs on cloth before it is dyed. The wax is removed after drying, leaving beautiful patterns. The young man is wearing *Adire* cloth, a unique fabric woven by his tribe.

Varied African Cuisine

There are many peoples in Africa, each with their own unique lifestyle and diet. For example, the nomadic Masai of East Africa herd cattle and consume a dairy-based diet. In contrast, the Bantu residing in southern Africa are an agricultural people, raising crops such as cassava, groundnuts, yams and spinach. Their diet is primarily vegetarian. Many regional culinary differences are apparent in the endless variations of Groundnut Stew, which are found throughout Africa.

Groundnut (Peanut) Stew

INGREDIENTS *(serves 4)*

1 chicken, quartered, skin removed
1 tablespoon vegetable oil
1 medium onion, chopped
1 green pepper, chopped
1 cup water
1/2 cup peanut butter
1 can (4 ounces) tomato paste
1 teaspoon grated fresh ginger
 (or 1/2 teaspoon ground ginger)
2 tablespoons brown sugar
1/8 teaspoon ground red pepper

DIRECTIONS

1 Prepare peanut sauce. In a bowl, combine the sugar, red pepper, ginger, peanut butter and tomato paste. Slowly stir in the water, a small amount at a time until the sauce is smooth. Set sauce aside.

2 Heat the oil in a large stew pot over a medium heat. Add the onion, cooking until it is translucent, approximately 5–7 minutes. Add the chicken and green pepper to the onion in the pot. Cook until chicken and onion are brown, and pepper is soft, approximately 20–25 minutes.

3 Pour the peanut sauce over the browned chicken, peppers and onions. Stir to combine. Cover the pot and reduce heat to low. Simmer, covered, for 1 hour, stirring occasionally.

4 Spoon servings of Groundnut Stew over Rice Balls (recipe follows), or on a bed of white rice.

Rice Balls

INGREDIENTS *(serves 4)*

1 cup short-grain white rice
3 1/2 cups water
1 teaspoon salt

DIRECTIONS

1 Prepare rice according to directions on package.

2 When rice is cooked, place it in a bowl. Using a potato masher or fork, mash rice until it begins to clump together. Set aside to cool.

3 Shape rice into balls. Fill a small bowl with cold water. Wet your hands with the cold water. Take a large handful of rice and shape it into a ball with your hands. Place the finished Rice Balls on a serving platter.

4 Rice Balls are traditionally served with soups or stews, such as Groundnut Stew (see facing page). Place one or two Rice Balls in the center of each serving bowl. Spoon the stew over the rice.

Africa: A Land of Many Climates

Africa, an extensive continent, boasts a dramatic variety of terrains and climates. Africa encompasses contrasting environs such as the hot arid Sahara Desert, the lush rainforest of the Zaire River Basin and the grassy savannah of Kenya. Perhaps the most remarkable geographical wonder is Mount Kilmanjaro, the highest peak in Africa. Although this renowned mountain is located just three degrees south of the fiery equator, its peak remains shrouded in glacial snow year round!

The Mortar and Pestle

In Africa, rice for this recipe is mashed using a mortar and pestle, such as the one shown in the illustration on page 8. The mortar (the wooden bowl) and the pestle (the long stick) are also used to mash yams or cassava, which are then shaped into balls called *Fufu*. The *Fufu* balls are served with soup or stew, in much the same way as Rice Balls are served. Groundnuts are also pulverized using the mortar and pestle for such dishes such as Groundnut Stew.

Greens Common in African Cuisine

COLLARDS: Frequently used in many West African dishes, collard greens are also a favorite of many African-American chefs, being readily available in the United States. These greens take longer than most to cook because they are quite tough when raw.

CASSAVA GREENS: The root of the cassava plant is commonly pounded into a dough for *Fufu*, a specialty in Ghana. African chefs utilize the green part as well.

CALLALOO: Callaloo greens come from the Taro plant and are often combined with tomato or peanuts in one-pot stews, in Caribbean cuisine as well as African.

Sautéed Spinach

INGREDIENTS *(serves 4)*

1 pound fresh spinach or other greens
1 small onion, finely chopped
1 large green pepper, seeded and coarsely chopped
1 can (4 ounces) tomato paste
2 teaspoons vegetable oil
salt and pepper to taste

DIRECTIONS

1 Wash greens well and drain.

2 Heat the oil in a large saucepan over medium heat.

3 Add the onion and cook until translucent, approximately 10 minutes. Add the peppers and cook until soft, approximately 5–7 minutes.

4 Add the spinach and tomato paste. Stir until combined.

5 Cover the pan and simmer 10 minutes, or until the spinach is wilted and heated throughout. Add salt and pepper to taste.

Is the Plant Mightier Than the Cow?

Much of African soil is unsuitable both for raising cattle and for agricultural use. While some Africans do raise cattle, the majority relies on farming for both commercial and subsistence food production. An acre of land cultivated with leafy greens produces 15 times more protein than the same area of land used for raising cattle. It is apparent that Africans make the most efficient use of their limited soil and resources.

Coconut Ice Cream

NOTE: This recipe requires an ice-cream maker.

INGREDIENTS *(serves 4-6)*

1 can (15 ounces) cream of coconut
1 cup superfine sugar
3 cups half and half
1 tablespoon coconut extract flavoring

DIRECTIONS

1 Mix sugar with cream of coconut in a medium-sized bowl until sugar is completely dissolved. Add the coconut extract flavoring.

2 Add the half and half, one cup at a time, stirring thoroughly with a spoon or a wire whisk until the mixture is smooth and well-blended.

3 Pour the mixture into your ice-cream maker and follow the processing instructions supplied by the manufacturer of the ice-cream maker.

Some Coffee with Your Ice Cream?

Kenya produces and exports some of the world's finest coffee. It is costly in the United States, yet some coffee connoisseurs agree it is well worth the higher price. Kenyan coffee is usually available at most gourmet coffee shops. Indulge for a special treat.

Is it Coconut Cream or Coconut Milk?

This recipe calls for cream of coconut, which is very sweet, rich and creamy, and suitable for desserts. Cream of coconut should not be confused with coconut milk, an ingredient used in many savory African main dishes. Coconut milk is not sweetened and is much lighter than cream of coconut. Be sure to read the label on the coconut product to ensure that you are purchasing the correct ingredient.

CARIBBEAN

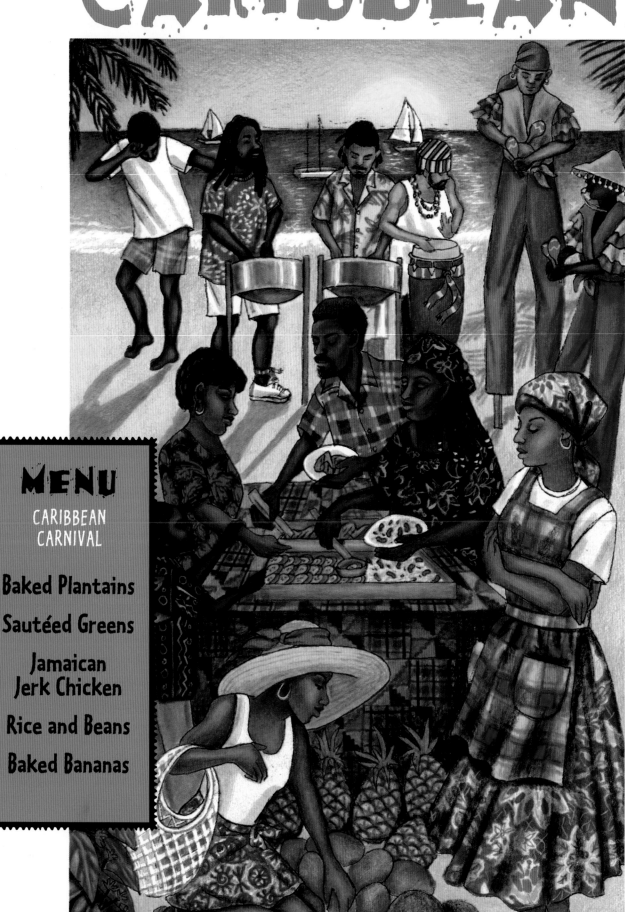

MENU

CARIBBEAN CARNIVAL

Baked Plantains

Sautéed Greens

Jamaican Jerk Chicken

Rice and Beans

Baked Bananas

Baked Plantains

INGREDIENTS *(serves 4)*

1/4 cup butter
2 tablespoons brown sugar
2 large ripe plantains

DIRECTIONS

1 Preheat oven to 375 degrees.

2 Prepare sauce. Mix the butter and brown sugar together in a small saucepan over low heat. Cook until the butter and sugar are completely melted and well blended. Set aside.

3 Cut the ends off both plantains and cut away the skin.

4 Cut the plantains into 1/2-inch slices.

5 Arrange the slices in a large shallow glass baking dish. Brush the sauce onto the plantain slices, using a pastry brush. Sprinkle with salt and pepper. Bake uncovered for 20–30 minutes, or until plantains are browned and glazed.

Caribbean Music, the Voice of the Islands

Reggae originated in Jamaica. The lyrics are often expressions of the Rastafarian values of freedom and peace. An international Reggae festival is held in Jamaica every August.

Calypso derives its name from the African word *Kaiso*, meaning verbal sparring. Its lyrics are often controversial, involving political and social statements.

Steel Band music was created in Trinidad by resourceful musicians using ordinary objects such as hub caps and pots to produce unique sounds. Eventually, these evolved into fine-tuned steel drums and pans. Trinidad holds a Steel Band Festival each October.

Carnival, Island-Style

While the well-known New Orleans Carnival is traditionally celebrated prior to Lent, it is held at varying times on the various islands of the Caribbean. During this festival, revelers sway to the rhythms of the Reggae, Calypso and Steel Band music flooding the streets and beaches. Jumby Dancers on stilts strut proudly in parades, showing off their dazzling costumes. Festive foods, such as Jamaican Jerk Chicken and Baked Plantains, are sold at stands lining the streets. The drawing on the facing page depicts Carnival, Island-Style.

Caribbean One-Pot Meals

In the Caribbean, the Sautéed Greens side dish featured on this page is often expanded into a one-pot meal known as callaloo or pepperpot. Just as the name of this dish varies among the Islands, so do the ingredients. Some versions are enriched with cured salted pork. Additional vegetables may include okra, green bell pepper and hot Scotch Bonnet Peppers. Extra water is added to pepperpot, making it more soup-like than callaloo, which is considered a stew. The common ingredient in all versions is greens such as spinach, kale, collards or callaloo. The use of callaloo greens inspired the name of the dish.

Sautéed Greens

INGREDIENTS *(serves 4)*

1 tablespoon vegetable oil
1 medium onion, chopped
2 garlic cloves, peeled and finely chopped
1 pound chopped, pre-washed fresh spinach
    or collard greens
salt and pepper to taste

DIRECTIONS

1 Heat the oil in a large skillet. Add the onion and cook 5–7 minutes, until soft and translucent.

2 Add the garlic to the onion in the pan and cook an additional 2–3 minutes.

3 Add the spinach or collard greens, stirring for approximately 2 minutes until all ingredients are combined. Cover and reduce heat to low. Simmer for 5 minutes, until greens are wilted and hot. Season with salt and pepper.

The Colorful Caribbean Market

Caribbean markets are bustling and lively. Island accents weave together as vendors hawk their wares and savvy shoppers bargain for the best price. Produce, from creamy yellow bananas to fuzzy brown coconuts, provides a tapestry of colors and textures. Caribbean chefs shop daily at local markets, basing their meals on whatever produce is especially fresh. The spirit of the Caribbean cuisine is to adapt the meals to the whims of nature and the availability of local resources.

Jamaican Jerk Chicken

INGREDIENTS *(serves 4)*

2 teaspoons ground allspice
1/2 teaspoon each of salt and black pepper
1/4 teaspoon ground red pepper
4 tablespoons dark brown sugar
2 tablespoons finely chopped fresh gingerroot
2 garlic cloves, peeled and finely chopped
1 medium onion, finely chopped
1 Scotch Bonnet Pepper, finely chopped
1/2 cup pineapple juice
1/3 cup each of balsamic vinegar, teriyaki sauce
    and vegetable oil
4 boneless, skinless chicken breasts

DIRECTIONS

1 The day before you plan to serve this dish, prepare the marinade. Combine allspice, salt, black pepper, red pepper, brown sugar, gingerroot, garlic, onion, Scotch Bonnet Pepper, pineapple juice, balsamic vinegar, teriyaki sauce and vegetable oil in a food processor until well blended.

2 Place the chicken breasts in a shallow glass baking pan. Reserve approximately 1/3 of the marinade for basting. Cover the chicken with the remaining marinade, turning to coat it on all sides. Cover the baking pan with plastic wrap and refrigerate overnight.

3 When you are ready to cook the chicken, preheat the oven to 350 degrees. Remove the plastic wrap and bake the chicken for 30 minutes.

4 Remove the chicken from the oven and grill it on an outdoor barbecue (or broil it indoors) for an additional 3–5 minutes on each side, brushing the chicken with the reserved marinade.

Jamaican Jerk, the Ancient Marinade

Jerk marinade was created by the Arawark Indians, the indigenous people of the Caribbean. The Arawark used the marinade to flavor and preserve their meat, usually wild boar, which is native to the mountains of Jamaica. The marinade utilizes Jamaican allspice, which is a single spice berry, not a combination of spices as its name suggests. Scotch Bonnet Peppers are known as *habanero* peppers in the southwest region of the United States. If *habaneros* are unavailable, jalapenos may be substituted.

Rice and Beans, the Universal Dish

In the Caribbean, Rice and Beans are served as a typical side dish. This dish, originally of Spanish origin, appears in the cuisines of other regions of the world, as well. The distinguishing element in each region is the type of beans used. Kidney beans are traditionally used in Spain. Pintos are the beans of choice in Mexico, while black beans are a Cuban specialty.

Rice and Beans

INGREDIENTS (serves 4)

1 tablespoon vegetable oil
1 onion, finely chopped
2 garlic cloves, finely chopped
1 cup uncooked long-grain white rice
1 can (approximately 15 ounces) kidney beans, drained
2 cups coconut milk
1/4 teaspoon crushed red pepper
1/2 teaspoon ground cumin
1/2 teaspoon salt

DIRECTIONS

1 Heat the oil in a large skillet over medium heat. Add the onion, cooking until golden brown, approximately 5–8 minutes.

2 Add the garlic to the onion in the skillet and cook 2–3 minutes longer.

3 Add the rice, beans, coconut milk, red pepper, cumin and salt. Stir until all ingredients are combined. Cover, reduce heat to simmer and cook for 20–30 minutes, stirring occasionally, until the rice is cooked and the liquid is absorbed.

The Caribbean, a Fusion of Diverse Cultures

British, Spanish, French and Dutch colonists, along with East Indian and West African laborers, brought their diverse cultures and cuisines to the Islands. These cultures and cuisines blended with those of the native Arawak Indians, yet each group left a lasting impression. Arawak jerk marinade, Indian curry, British cricket and the African-inspired Reggae survived the centuries to form the basis of today's Caribbean culture and cuisine.

Baked Bananas

INGREDIENTS *(serves 4)*

1/2 cup whipped cream cheese
2 tablespoons butter, softened
1/4 cup brown sugar
1 teaspoon ground cinnamon
1 tablespoon rum (optional)
1 teaspoon vanilla extract
1/4 cup coconut milk or heavy cream
4 ripe bananas
1/4 cup shredded coconut

DIRECTIONS

1 Preheat over to 350 degrees.

2 Blend the cream cheese, butter, brown sugar, cinnamon, rum (if desired), vanilla extract and coconut milk or heavy cream in a blender or food processor until smooth. Set aside.

3 Peel the bananas and slice in half lengthwise. Arrange the bananas in a single layer in a greased glass baking dish.

4 Spread the cream-cheese mixture evenly over the bananas. Sprinkle shredded coconut over the cream-cheese-covered bananas.

5 Bake for 20–25 minutes or until lightly brown and bubbly. Serve hot.

Martinique, the Banana Capital of the Caribbean

The balmy tropical climate of the Caribbean is conducive to growing a variety of fruits, especially bananas and coconuts. The island of Martinique has such a prolific banana crop that much of it can be exported. The Baked Bananas recipe on this page is said to have its origin in Martinique, the banana capital of the Caribbean.

CHINA

MENU

CHINESE NEW YEAR CELEBRATION

Egg Drop Soup

Cold Sesame Noodles

Chinese Spare Ribs

Chicken with Cashews

Fried Rice

Egg Drop Soup

INGREDIENTS *(serves 4)*

3 tablespoons cold water
1 tablespoon cornstarch
1 egg
4 cups canned chicken broth
2 scallions, finely chopped, including the green part

DIRECTIONS

1 Place the cold water in a small cup. Stir in the cornstarch. Be sure to stir any lumps out. Set aside.

2 Break the egg into a small bowl and beat well. Set aside.

3 Heat the chicken broth in a medium-sized soup pot until it begins to boil. Slowly add the cornstarch mixture into the broth and boil an additional minute or two, stirring constantly with a spoon, until broth is slightly thickened.

4 Slowly stir in the beaten egg with a fork. The egg will form long ribbon-like strands.

5 Pour into serving bowls and garnish with the chopped scallion.

Fooling Evil Spirits

While there are a multitude of rituals designed to usher in good luck for the New Year, there are also numerous customs intended to keep evil spirits at bay. For example, on the first day of the New Year, it is customary to wear new clothing in order to keep from being recognized by evil spirits, which would bring the wearer bad luck in the coming year.

Chinese New Year Celebrations

Chinese New Year is celebrated from the end of January through the beginning of February. The focus of the festivities is to ensure good luck in the coming year. The Lion Dance, which appears in the upper right of the illustration on the facing page, is an important ritual. Two or three dancers, concealed under an elaborate lion costume, roam the streets. Revelers and shop owners give the lion red envelopes containing money to ensure a prosperous new year.

Cold Sesame Noodles

INGREDIENTS *(serves 4)*

1/4 cup soy sauce
1/4 cup brown sugar
2 tablespoons rice vinegar
1 tablespoon sesame oil
1/2 cup creamy peanut butter
1/4 cup tahini (sesame paste)
1 tablespoon sesame seeds
4 scallions, finely chopped, including the green part
8 ounces soba noodles (Soba noodles can be found in Asian grocery stores. If soba noodles are unavailable, spaghetti may be substituted.)

DIRECTIONS

1 Prepare sesame sauce. Combine the soy sauce and brown sugar in a small saucepan and bring to a boil over medium heat, stirring constantly. Turn off heat and allow to cool slightly. Combine the soy/sugar mixture, rice vinegar, sesame oil, peanut butter and tahini in a blender or food processor until smooth. Set aside.

2 Boil the soba noodles according to the directions on the box—do not overcook. When noodles are done, place in a colander and immediately put under cold running water. Continue rinsing until all noodles are cool.

3 Drain the pasta well and place in a large bowl. Pour the sesame sauce on top, add the scallions and stir until the noodles are well coated. Sprinkle with sesame seeds and refrigerate for several hours before serving.

Chinese Spare Ribs

INGREDIENTS *(serves 4)*

1/4 cup soy sauce
1/2 cup hoisin sauce (available in the Asian section
   of your supermarket)
1 garlic clove, minced
1/2 cup honey
1/4 cup ketchup or chili sauce (use chili sauce for
   a spicy result)
2 pounds baby back spare ribs

DIRECTIONS

1 The day before you plan to serve this dish, prepare the marinade. Mix the soy sauce, hoisin sauce and garlic together in a small bowl.

2 Place the ribs in a glass baking pan and cover with the marinade, turning the ribs to coat on all sides. Cover with foil and marinate in refrigerator overnight.

3 To cook the ribs, preheat the oven to 350 degrees. Bake, still covered with the foil, for 30 minutes.

4 While the ribs are baking, prepare the finishing glaze. Combine honey and ketchup or chili sauce in a small bowl and set aside.

5 After the ribs have baked for 30 minutes, remove the baking pan from the oven. Baste the ribs on both sides with the finishing glaze, using a pastry brush.

6 Return the ribs to the oven, increase heat to 400 degrees and bake uncovered for an additional 20 minutes, until ribs are glazed and browned.

Chinese Zodiac

The Chinese Zodiac, featured in the drawing on page 20, is an important part of the Chinese New Year. Each of the twelve animals in the zodiac represents specific years. It is believed that the individuals posses characteristics of the animal under whose sign they were born. It is particularly lucky to be born in the year of the dragon. While in Western culture, dragons traditionally have an evil image, in China they symbolize good luck.

Chicken with Cashews

INGREDIENTS *(serves 4)*

4 boneless, skinless chicken breasts,
    cut into bite-sized cubes
1 teaspoon cornstarch
1/4 cup soy sauce
1/4 cup cooking sherry
1 tablespoon honey
1 teaspoon rice wine vinegar
1 teaspoon sesame oil
1 red pepper, cut into bite-sized squares
1 small onion, coarsely chopped
2 scallions, finely chopped, including the green part
1/2 cup unsalted cashews
2 garlic cloves, finely chopped
1 small piece (size of a walnut) fresh gingerroot,
    peeled and very finely chopped

DIRECTIONS

1 Prepare sauce. In a small bowl mix the cornstarch and soy sauce together until smooth. Stir in the sherry, honey and rice vinegar. Set aside.

2 Heat the sesame oil in a wok or large frying pan over high heat. When the oil is very hot, add the onion and chicken, stirring until all the chicken is cooked and brown, and the onion is soft (about 5–7 minutes). Add the peppers, garlic, scallions, ginger and cashews, cooking an additional 3–5 minutes.

3 Add the sauce and continue cooking until it thickens (about 3–5 minutes), stirring constantly.

Fried Rice

INGREDIENTS *(serves 4)*

2 tablespoons sesame oil
1/2 onion, finely chopped
2 scallions, finely chopped, including the green part
1/4 cup canned peas
1/4 cup soy sauce
2 eggs, beaten well
2 cups cooked day-old white rice (The cooked rice should
    be refrigerated for an entire day, so that it will form
    appetizing clumps when fried.)

DIRECTIONS

1 Heat the oil in a large wok or skillet over medium-high heat. Add the onion, cooking 2–3 minutes or until soft.

2 Add the rice, stirring constantly, cooking until lightly brown, about 5 minutes.

3 Stir in the peas, scallions and soy sauce.

4 Using a spoon, make a hole in the center of the rice mixture. Pour the eggs into the hole and cook until they begin to set. Then stir the eggs into the remaining mixture. Stir until the eggs are completely cooked and blended with the rice.

All the Rice in China

Almost half the population in China earns its living by farming. The most abundant crop is rice, which is considered the staple of the Chinese diet. At breakfast, rice is made into porridge called *congee*. Lunch and dinner consist of a bowl of rice with one or two side dishes of meat, tofu or vegetables. At special occasions, many side dishes are served. Each guest receives a bowl of rice, while the side dishes are placed in the center of the table for all the guests to share.

Pasta was invented in...China?

In addition to rice, wheat is an important crop in China. It is made into a variety of noodles and dumplings. Some historical documents indicate that noodles were in fact invented in China, not in Italy as commonly believed. Marco Polo is said to have brought the noodle recipe to Italy after a journey to China in the 13th century.

France

Menu
BASTILLE DAY PICNIC

Cheese and Fruit Plate

Smoked Salmon Mousse

Onion Tarte

Salade Niçoise

French Silk Pie

Cheese and Fruit Plate

INGREDIENTS *(serves 4)*

1/4 pound Brie cheese
1/4 pound Camembert cheese
1/4 pound herbed Chèvre (goat cheese)
1 green Granny Smith apple
1 tablespoon fresh lemon juice
1/4 pound red grapes
1 package of fancy crackers

DIRECTIONS

1 Unwrap the Brie, Camembert and Chèvre cheeses and place in the center of an attractive serving platter.

2 Remove the core from the apple. Cut the apple into thin slices, keeping the skin on. Sprinkle the slices with the lemon juice to prevent browning. Surround the cheese decoratively with the apple slices.

3 Add the grapes and crackers to the serving platter, taking care to make a beautiful appetizing display. Set a knife nearby for slicing the cheese.

Fruit and Cheese...For Dessert?

Fruit and cheese are often served for dessert in France. In France, cheeses are named after the province in which they originated. Brie and Camembert are two of the most famous provinces that have been making cheeses for centuries. The many French cheeses—Brie in particular—are soft and creamy and have a high fat content. It is easy to understand why this rich decadent treat is considered a dessert!

Bastille Day

Bastille Day, or French Independence Day, is also known as *Le Quatorze Juillet* **because it is celebrated on July 14. The French celebrate Bastille Day in much the same way Americans celebrate Independence Day on July 4: with parades, parties, fireworks and, of course,** *pique-niques*, **such as the one illustrated on the facing page. The tri-colored flag waves proudly throughout the nation:** *Vive la France!*

How to Fold Whipped Cream into a Mousse

Stir a big spoonful of whipped cream into the mousse mixture to lighten it. Spoon the remaining cream on top of the mousse mixture. Using a rubber spatula, cut down to the bottom of the bowl and bring some of the mousse mixture to the surface, up and over the whipped cream. Repeat this motion, rotating the bowl until the mousse mixture is just blended with the cream. Do not over-blend, as this will cause the cream to fall.

Smoked Salmon Mousse

INGREDIENTS *(serves 8)*

1 envelope unflavored gelatin
1/4 cup cold water
1/2 cup boiling water
1/2 cup whipped cream cheese
1 pound smoked salmon
1/2 cup mayonnaise
1 tablespoon freshly squeezed lemon juice
1/2 teaspoon paprika
1 pinch ground red pepper
1/4 cup scallions, finely sliced, including the green part
1 cup heavy whipping cream

DIRECTIONS

1 Pour the cold water into a small bowl and sprinkle with gelatin. Stir well and set aside for 3 minutes. Add the boiling water and stir until gelatin is dissolved. Cool until it reaches room temperature.

2 Prepare the mousse mixture. Place the smoked salmon, the cooled gelatin mixture and the cream cheese in a food processor or blender to puree. Pour the pureed mixture into a bowl and stir in the mayonnaise, lemon juice, paprika, red pepper and scallions. Refrigerate 30 minutes, until mixture begins to thicken.

3 Prepare whipped cream. In a medium-sized chilled bowl, whip the cream with an electric beater or mixer until stiff peaks form.

4 Gently fold the whipped cream into the thickened mousse mixture (see sidebar). Pour the final blended mixture into an attractive serving bowl and refrigerate at least 4 hours.

Onion Tarte

INGREDIENTS *(serves 6–8)*

1 package (2 pounds) frozen bread dough
2 teaspoons olive oil
2 large onions, thinly sliced
2 tablespoons granulated brown sugar
1/4 teaspoon salt
1 pinch ground black pepper
1 small can (2 ounces) anchovies

DIRECTIONS

1 Thaw bread dough. Preheat oven to 400 degrees.

2 Grease a large (at least 10 by 15 inches) cookie sheet with a little butter. Using a rolling pin, roll the dough out into a large rectangle and place into the greased cookie sheet. Lightly press the dough to cover the entire pan.

3 Heat the oil in a large skillet over medium heat. Add the onions and sprinkle them with brown sugar, salt and pepper. Cook until the onions are caramelized. (The onions are caramelized when they become soft, brown and sticky. The caramelizing process should take approximately 20 minutes.)

4 Spread the caramelized onions evenly over the rolled dough. Arrange the anchovies in a crisscross pattern over the onions. The crisscross pattern can be clearly seen on the bread in the illustration on page 26.

5 Bake uncovered until the tarte is lightly brown, about 20–25 minutes. Cool approximately 10 minutes. Cut into squares and serve.

French Specialty Shops

In France, onion tartes, or *pissaladières*, as the French call them, are sold in *boulangeries*. A *boulangerie* is a French bakery specializing in breads such as croissants, baguettes and brioche. A *boulangerie* is just one of the many specialty shops that thrive in France. There are also *charcuteries* that offer sausages and meats, while *fromageries* specialize only in cheese. The French prefer to frequent these small shops instead of large supermarkets.

Nice, the Birthplace of the Salade Niçoise

Salade Niçoise was originally created in Nice, a charming and sophisticated resort town on the French Riviera, also known as *La Côte d'Azur*. Most likely, the dish was created at one of the many chic cafés scattered throughout Nice. The salad was eventually named "Niçoise" in honor of its birthplace.

Salade Niçoise

INGREDIENTS *(serves 4)*

Salad

1 garlic clove, peeled and cut in half
1 head iceberg lettuce, washed and cut into small pieces
1/2 red onion, peeled and cut into thin slices
2 tomatoes, washed and cut into wedges
1 can tuna (4 1/2 ounces), drained
10 black olives, coarsely chopped

French Vinaigrette

1/4 cup extra virgin olive oil
2 tablespoons red wine vinegar (Shallot or tarragon vinegar may be used in place of red wine vinegar.)
1 teaspoon Dijon mustard
1 teaspoon sugar
juice from 1/2 lemon

DIRECTIONS

1 Cut garlic clove in half and rub the cut surface on the inside of a wooden salad bowl.

2 Place the lettuce in the salad bowl. Arrange the red onion and tomato on top of the lettuce. Spoon the tuna in the center of the salad. Garnish with black olives.

3 Prepare the dressing. Combine the olive oil, wine vinegar, mustard, sugar and lemon juice using a wire whisk, food processor or blender. Pour over salad and serve.

French Silk Pie

INGREDIENTS *(serves 8)*

1 container (8 ounces) whipped cream cheese
1/2 cup unsweetened cocoa
1 cup powdered confectioner's sugar
2 cups heavy whipping cream
1 ready-made graham-cracker pie crust

DIRECTIONS

1 In a large bowl, beat the cream cheese and cocoa until well-blended.

2 Add the powdered sugar, a small amount at a time, until it is blended into the mixture.

3 In a small bowl, whip the heavy cream with a hand-held electric mixer on high speed until stiff. Gently fold the whipped cream into the cheese and cocoa mixture, taking care to keep the whipped cream fluffy. Pour into piecrust and refrigerate for several hours before serving. If desired, decorate with additional whipped cream.

Are you a Gourmet, or a Gourmand?

Although the French words *gourmet* and *gourmand* are very similar, they have very different meanings. A *gourmet* is an individual who savors fine food and spirits with a discriminating taste. The word was derived from the French word *gromet*, meaning the groom or keeper of the wine cellar. A *gourmand* is an individual who overindulges in fine food to excess. Note the similarities to the words gorge and glutton!

Aspire to be a Gourmet, not a Gourmand! Bon Appétit!

The Patissier

The preparation of fine food in France is taken very seriously. Pastry making in particular is considered an art form. A chef studies for many years to become a *patissier*, or pastry chef. A *patissier*'s craft is showcased in cafés, fine restaurants and *patisseries* (French pastry shops). The French culinary community has earned its distinguished reputation with magnificent desserts such as petits fours, mille-feuilles and chocolate mousse.

Germany

Menu

OKTOBERFEST!

Bavarian
Bratwurst

Red Cabbage

German
Potato Salad

Green Beans
with Spaetzle

Apple Strudel

Bavarian Bratwurst

INGREDIENTS *(serves 4)*

1 large onion
1 tablespoon butter
4 bratwurst sausages
4 hard sandwich rolls

DIRECTIONS

1 Peel onion and cut into thin slices.

2 Melt butter in a large skillet and add onion slices. Cook over medium heat until onions are soft, about 5–10 minutes.

3 Add the bratwurst and cook over medium heat until brown, approximately 20–30 minutes. Turn bratwurst and onions as you cook them, so they will brown evenly.

4 Slice sandwich rolls. Place one bratwurst and some onions in each roll. If you like sauerkraut, omit the onions and top your bratwurst with sauerkraut instead.

Oktoberfest: It's Not Just Beer!

Oktoberfest began in Munich as a festival for the October beers, which were now ready for drinking after aging over the summer. However the true focus of Oktoberfest is camaraderie among people coming together to enjoy fine food and drink. A German Brass Oompah band, such as the one featured on the facing page, provides music for the fest. Clad in lederhosen and dirndls, the musicians stomp and blare through the streets and beer halls of Munich, bringing merriment to all.

Cabbage in Germany

Cabbage, or *kraut*, as Germans call it, is one of the distinctive ingredients in German cuisine. Sauerkraut, the best-known German cabbage dish, is made by salting and fermenting shredded white cabbage. White cabbage is also used in coleslaw, the quintessential salad of Germany. Red cabbage is often prepared in a sweet and sour (or *broken söt*) manner, as in the recipe on this page. It is served as a piquant side dish with German sausage and other meat dishes.

Red Cabbage

INGREDIENTS *(serves 4)*

2 tablespoons vegetable oil
1 onion, peeled and sliced thin
2 tablespoons granulated brown sugar
1 head (about 2 pounds) of red cabbage, stem removed, shredded
1 apple, peeled and sliced
1 tablespoon salt
6 whole cloves
1/2 cup red wine
1/4 cup balsamic vinegar
1/4 cup red wine vinegar
5 tablespoons red currant jelly

DIRECTIONS

1 Heat the oil in a large skillet over medium heat. Add the onion and brown sugar. Sauté approximately 5 minutes, until onion is soft.

2 Add the cabbage and apple to the skillet. Sauté for several additional minutes, until cabbage, apple and onion are coated evenly with the oil and sugar.

3 Stir in the salt, cloves, red wine, balsamic and red wine vinegars. Cover and simmer over low heat for 1 hour.

4 Stir in red currant jelly and simmer, uncovered, for an additional 30–45 minutes or until cabbage is tender. Remove cloves before serving.

German Potato Salad

INGREDIENTS *(serves 4)*

2 pounds red potatoes, not peeled
5 strips smoked bacon, cut into 1-inch pieces
1 small onion, chopped fine
1 teaspoon all purpose white flour
1 tablespoon sugar
6 tablespoons cider vinegar
1 tablespoon Dijon mustard
1/2 teaspoon salt
1/2 cup water
1 tablespoon chopped parsley

DIRECTIONS

1 Bring a medium-sized pot of salted water to boil. Add the unpeeled potatoes and boil until they are tender, about 30 minutes. Remove potatoes from water. When potatoes are cool enough to handle, peel and cut into thin slices.

2 Fry the bacon in a large skillet until it is crisp. Remove and drain on paper towels. Leave the remaining bacon fat in the skillet.

3 Prepare dressing. Add the chopped onion to the bacon fat in the skillet. Sauté over medium heat for 5 minutes, until onion is soft. Stir the flour into the bacon fat/onion mixture, cooking 2–3 minutes. Stir in sugar, vinegar, mustard and salt until mixture is smooth. Slowly add the water, cooking an additional 3–5 minutes, until thickened. Add the cooked bacon to the dressing.

4 Pour the dressing over the potatoes, tossing gently until coated. Sprinkle with parsley. Serve warm.

Potatoes, the "Ground Pear" of Germany

The humble potato, also known as the "ground pear" or "earth apple" in Germany, forms the basis of many of Germany's most famous contributions to the culinary world. Potato pancakes, potato dumplings and German Potato Salad are just a few of the renowned dishes. Remember that German Potato Salad is always served warm, a tradition carried on since olden times, when the salad was kept near the hearth to maintain its warmth.

Green Beans with Spaetzle

INGREDIENTS *(serves 4)*

1 pound fresh green beans, with ends cut
2 eggs, beaten
1 cup all purpose white flour
1/4 cup whole milk
1/2 teaspoon salt
dash of black pepper
1/4 teaspoon baking powder
1/4 cup salted butter

DIRECTIONS

1 Fill a large saucepan with salted water and bring to boil.

2 Prepare the spaetzle batter. Beat eggs in a small bowl. Stir in the flour, milk, salt, pepper and baking powder until well combined.

3 Press batter through a colander, a small amount at a time, into the boiling water. (This will create the traditional squiggle-shaped spaetzle.) Lower heat and simmer for about 5 minutes, stirring occasionally to make sure the spaetzle don't stick to the bottom. When the spaetzle are done they will float to the surface. Remove them from the water with a slotted spoon.

4 Melt the butter in a large frying pan. Add the green beans and sauté until they are bright green—lightly cooked, but still slightly crispy—about 2–3 minutes. Add the cooked spaetzle and gently cook another 2–3 minutes, until the spaetzle are warm and evenly coated with the butter.

Apple Strudel

INGREDIENTS *(serves 4-6)*

1 sheet frozen puff pastry
4 green Granny Smith apples
1/4 cup brown sugar
2 teaspoons ground cinnamon
1/2 cup whole shelled walnuts
1/4 cup dark raisins
1 egg, well beaten
1/4 cup finely chopped walnuts for garnish

DIRECTIONS

1 Preheat oven to 400 degrees.

2 Thaw the frozen puff pastry while preparing the apple mixture. To prepare apple mixture, peel the apples, remove the cores and slice thin. Combine the sliced apples with the sugar, cinnamon, walnuts and raisins in a large bowl.

3 Open the sheet of thawed pastry on a cutting board or other flat surface. If pastry is too stiff to handle, allow it to thaw a little longer, until it is pliable and easy to handle. Spread the apple mixture evenly over the single sheet of pastry. Roll up carefully, like a jelly roll, being careful not to roll too tightly, since the dough will expand during the baking process.

4 Gently place the strudel on a greased baking pan, seam side down. Brush top with beaten egg, then sprinkle with chopped walnuts. Bake for 20 minutes at 400 degrees. Reduce heat to 350 degrees and bake another 10-15 minutes or until golden brown.

German Desserts, the Sunday Treat

In Germany, desserts are traditionally enjoyed on weekends and holidays only. In contemplating the array of rich German desserts, it is easy to understand why they are reserved as a special treat! These decadent delights range from Black Forest cake to heavenly Bavarian cream to endless varieties of strudel, including apple, cherry and cheese. It is amusing to note that the German translation of strudel is whirlpool, referring to the elaborate rolling of the pastry around delectable fillings.

GREECE

MENU

ATHENIAN
FEAST

Greek Salad

Spanikopita

Moussaka

Vasilopita Bread

Baklava

Greek Salad

INGREDIENTS *(serves 4)*

1 head romaine lettuce, torn into bite-sized pieces
2 tomatoes, cut in wedges
1 cucumber, thinly sliced
1 sweet onion, thinly sliced
1 green pepper, finely diced
1 can (4 ounces) black olives
1/2 cup crumbled feta cheese
1/4 cup extra virgin olive oil
juice of 1 lemon
2 tablespoons red wine vinegar
1/2 teaspoon sugar
1/2 teaspoon salt
1 teaspoon dried oregano
freshly ground pepper

DIRECTIONS

1 Layer the lettuce, tomatoes, cucumber, onion, green pepper, olives and feta cheese in a large salad bowl.

2 Combine the olive oil, lemon juice, vinegar, oregano, salt and sugar in a small jar that has a snug-fitting lid. Cover tightly with the lid and shake hard until the dressing is well mixed.

3 Pour the dressing over the salad and toss gently until salad is well coated. Lightly sprinkle with freshly ground pepper before serving.

Lemons in Greek Cuisine

Fragrant lemon trees are abundant throughout the hills of Greece. It is no wonder that lemon is a favorite flavoring in many Greek recipes.

Dramatic Greek Folk Dancing

The children illustrated on the facing page are performing a Greek folk dance known as the *Syritaki*. The *Syritaki* is an expressive line dance, performed to dramatic and soulful *bouzouki* music. Wearing traditional Greek costumes, the dancers cavort in an exuberant frenzy with their arms around each other in a gesture of camaraderie. Every so often a single dancer, inspired by the music, will break from a group to perform a solo, featuring skillful and energetic kicks.

Mezethes, Greek Hors d'Oeurves

In Greece, lunch is eaten at 2 p.m., while dinner never starts before 9 p.m. Hors d'oeurves called *mezethes* fill the large span between meals. These tantalizing snacks may include small amounts of stuffed grape leaves, caviar dip and Spanikopita. *Mezethes* are served in Greek cafés known as tavernas. These lively establishments set their tables in patios and courtyards and even on rooftops! Many tavernas offer live entertainment and stay open late into the evening.

Spanikopita

INGREDIENTS *(serves 6-8)*

1 pound phyllo pastry dough

2 bags (10 ounces each) fresh spinach (2 6-ounce packages of frozen chopped spinach may be substituted. Thaw the spinach and drain well.)

8 scallions, finely chopped, including the green part

2 tablespoons finely chopped fresh dill

2 large eggs, lightly beaten

8 ounces feta cheese

1/2 cup olive oil

DIRECTIONS

1 Preheat oven to 350 degrees.

2 Prepare spinach filling. Wash the spinach thoroughly and drain. Chop the spinach in a food processor. Mix the spinach, scallions, dill, eggs and feta cheese in a large bowl.

3 Lay a sheet of phyllo dough in a greased baking pan (9 by 13 inches) and brush the top of the sheet with a little olive oil, using a pastry brush. Add five more phyllo sheets, one at a time, brushing a little of the oil on top of each one.

4 Spread half the spinach mixture over the phyllo dough. Layer four additional sheets of phyllo on top, brushing each sheet with oil. Add the rest of the spinach mixture and cover with 5-6 more layers of phyllo dough, again brushing each layer with oil.

5 Using a knife or pizza cutter, cut into 8-10 squares.

6 Bake for 40 minutes, or until top is golden. Remove from oven and allow to cool for 10-15 minutes. Serve warm.

Moussaka

INGREDIENTS *(serves 6–8)*

1 cup corn oil or olive oil for frying
1 small eggplant, cut into 1/2-inch slices
1 medium onion, finely chopped
1 pound ground lamb or beef
1 can (14 ounces) tomato sauce
1 stick butter
1/2 cup flour
2 cups milk
2 eggs slightly beaten
1 cup grated Greek Kefalotiri cheese (1 cup grated
     parmesan cheese may be substituted)
2 potatoes, peeled, boiled for 15 minutes and thinly sliced

DIRECTIONS

1 Preheat oven to 400 degrees.

2 Heat the oil in a large skillet over medium heat. Add the eggplant, a few slices at a time, until lightly brown on both sides. Drain the cooked slices on paper towels.

3 Cook the onion and meat in a skillet until brown. Drain off extra fat. Add tomato sauce and simmer for 20 minutes.

4 Prepare Bechamel sauce. Melt the butter in a large saucepan over low heat. Stir in the flour with a whisk, then add the milk a little at a time, whisking constantly. Cook until thickened, then remove from heat and stir in 1/2 cup of the Kefalotiri cheese. Beat in the eggs.

5 Cover the bottom of a large greased baking pan with eggplant. Layer the meat on top of the eggplant. Repeat to create several layers of eggplant and meat, then top with potato slices.

6 Pour the Bechamel sauce on top, and sprinkle with the remaining cheese. Bake for 30–40 minutes. Cool for 10 minutes before serving.

The Ancient City of Athens

Modern-day Athens still bears evidence of its fabled past. The heart of the city is the Acropolis. Perched high on a rocky hill, it is the distinguished home of four ancient buildings, which have stood there since the 5th century B.C. The most sacred is the temple of Athena, known as the Parthenon, the building seen in the illustration on page 38. Legend has it that Zeus appointed Athena goddess of Athens because she created the first olive tree. Today, Greek olives are considered the finest in the world.

Why Is a Coin Inserted into the Bread?

Traditionally, in Greece, a coin is inserted into this bread to celebrate the New Year. The bread is sliced at the stroke of midnight on New Year's Eve. A slice of bread is cut for every member of the family, beginning with the oldest family member, and ending with the youngest. It is believed that the family member who finds the coin in their slice of bread will have good luck in the new year.

Vasilopita Bread

INGREDIENTS *(makes one large loaf)*

1 cup milk

2 packages yeast

10 cups all purpose white flour

6 eggs

1 teaspoon salt

1/2 pound butter (2 sticks), melted

1 1/2 cups white sugar

1 teaspoon ground *mahlepi* dissolved in 1/4 cup warm water (*Mahlepi* is a ground spice berry, available in some Greek import shops.)

DIRECTIONS

1 Preheat oven to 375 degrees.

2 Prepare the yeast mixture. Heat the milk to lukewarm in a small saucepan over low heat. Pour the warmed milk into a small bowl containing the yeast, stirring until dissolved. Add 1/4 cup of the flour, mixing until well blended. Cover mixture with foil and set it in a warm place to rise for 30 minutes.

3 In a large bowl, combine 4 eggs, salt, butter, sugar, *mahlepi*, risen yeast mixture and the remaining flour. Knead this dough on a floured surface until it is smooth. Return dough to the bowl, cover with foil and set in a warm place until the dough doubles in bulk, about 2 hours.

4 Punch down the dough and press into a round greased baking pan. Cover with foil and allow it to rise again, for about 1 hour.

5 Beat the remaining 2 eggs and brush them on top of the bread with a pastry brush.

6 Bake for 15 minutes, then reduce heat to 300 degrees and bake for 25 more minutes. Cool, then insert coin (see sidebar).

Baklava

INGREDIENTS *(makes about 20 pieces)*

1 pound shelled walnuts, chopped
2 tablespoons granulated brown sugar
1 teaspoon cinnamon
1 pound frozen phyllo pastry, thawed
1 stick unsalted butter, melted
1 cup honey
1 cup water

DIRECTIONS

1 Preheat oven to 350 degrees.

2 In a medium bowl, mix the walnuts, sugar and cinnamon.

3 Assemble the baklava. Place one sheet of phyllo pastry in a greased glass baking pan large enough to hold phyllo sheets (approximately 9 by 13 inches). Brush the sheet with a small amount of the melted butter.

4 Add 5 more phyllo sheets, brushing each one with butter. Top with 1/3 of nut mixture. Add another 3 phyllo sheets, again brushing each sheet with butter.

5 Repeat step 3 twice, until all of the nut mixture has been used. Then top with the remaining 5–7 sheets of phyllo dough, each brushed with butter.

6 Cut the top layers into diamond-shaped pieces, using a knife or a pizza cutter. (Do not cut through the bottom layers.)

7 Bake until golden brown, approximately 50 minutes. Remove from oven and cool.

8 Bring honey and water to a boil in a saucepan over medium heat. Boil for 10 minutes. Pour syrup over the cooled baklava. Cool to room temperature before cutting and serving.

Tips for Working with Phyllo Dough

Working with delicate phyllo (which means leaf in Greek) requires patience and practice. Here are some tips to make it easier.

Thaw frozen phyllo in the refrigerator, not at room temperature. Allow 8 hours for the phyllo to defrost.

Phyllo dries out very quickly once it is unwrapped. You will have to work rapidly, so have all other ingredients prepared before assembling your phyllo creation. Cover phyllo sheets that are waiting to be used with plastic wrap to retain moisture.

India

Menu
A BANQUET IN BOMBAY

Cucumbers
in Yogurt

Couscous

Tandoori Chicken

Shrimp Curry

Mango Pudding

Cucumbers in Yogurt

INGREDIENTS *(serves 4)*

1 cucumber
2 scallions, finely chopped, including the green part
1 cup plain yogurt
2 tablespoons chopped fresh mint or cilantro
1 teaspoon salt
1/2 teaspoon superfine sugar
juice of 1 lemon

DIRECTIONS

1 Peel and thinly slice cucumber.

2 Prepare yogurt dressing. Mix the yogurt, mint or cilantro, salt, sugar and lemon juice in a medium-sized bowl.

3 Add the cucumber and scallion; stir to combine.

4 Cover with plastic wrap and refrigerate for one hour before serving.

Cooling Yogurt Dishes

The refreshing cold yogurt and vegetable dish on this page is called a *raita* in Indian cuisine. *Raitas* complement the hot pungent aspect of Indian meals by taking the sting out of the fiery spices and chili peppers liberally used in many typical dishes. A *raita* is commonly served after a spicy dish such as Shrimp Curry, to cleanse and soothe the diner's palate.

Ornamentation, the Art of India

The illustration on the facing page represents India's love of color, detail and decoration. Indian people take pleasure in adorning their homes, themselves and even their animals. The richly hued, intricately detailed carpets crafted in India are works of art. Women's saris are hand-embroidered with delicate designs and tiny mirrors. Elephants are often draped with brightly embellished covers. It is not surprising that the extravagantly colored peacock is the national bird of India.

Vegetarian Tradition in India

Couscous is one of the many grains grown in India. Grains play an essential role in Indian cuisine since many Indians are vegetarian, in keeping with the Hindu belief that animals are sacred and not for consumption. While couscous can be served as a side dish to chicken or seafood, in many regions of India it is prepared as a vegetarian main dish. Legumes, such as lentils, and a variety of vegetables are added, making it a complete and nutritious meal.

Couscous

INGREDIENTS *(serves 4)*

1 cup canned chicken broth
1/2 teaspoon turmeric
1/2 teaspoon curry
1/2 teaspoon cinnamon
1 cup couscous (You can find couscous in
    the rice section of a supermarket.)
1/4 cup sliced almonds for garnish (optional)

DIRECTIONS

1 Heat the chicken broth in a saucepan over medium-high heat.

2 Add the turmeric, curry and cinnamon, stirring to blend.

3 Reduce heat to low and slowly stir in the couscous. Continue to cook over low heat, stirring constantly until most of the liquid is absorbed. This should take several minutes.

4 Turn off heat. Cover the saucepan and let stand for about 10–15 minutes, until all the liquid is absorbed.

5 Fluff with a fork before serving. Garnish with almond slices.

Basmati Rice, an Exotic Side Dish

In addition to couscous, Basmati rice is a typical side dish served in India. This exotic long-grain rice is grown exclusively in the foothills of the Himalayan Mountains. The most notable feature of this rice is its nutty fragrance. Basmati is aged for one year to heighten its aroma, which makes it quite expensive. It can be found in the United States in gourmet shops and Middle Eastern grocery stores. Be sure to read the directions on the package carefully; Basmati rice usually requires rinsing and soaking prior to cooking.

Tandoori Chicken

INGREDIENTS *(serves 4)*

2 tablespoons tandoori paste (You can find this is the
gourmet/ethnic food section of most supermarkets.)
1/2 cup plain (unflavored) yogurt
2 garlic cloves, peeled and minced
4 chicken leg quarters

The Tandoor Oven

Tandoori paste turns chicken a beautiful red color. This distinctive color comes from the fiery red chilies that are ground into the tandoori paste. The recipe, however, does not derive its name from this spicy paste, but from the clay-lined tandoor oven used in India. In the traditional Indian tandoori method, chicken or seafood is first marinated in a chili and yogurt mixture similar to the one in the Tandoori Chicken recipe here. It is then cooked in the tandor, over hot coals.

DIRECTIONS

1 The day before you plan to cook the chicken, prepare the tandoori marinade. Mix the tandoori paste with the yogurt and garlic until smooth.

2 Remove the skin from the chicken and discard it. Place the chicken in a glass baking dish. Pour the tandoori marinade over the chicken. Using a pastry brush, coat the pieces of chicken on all sides with the marinade. Cover the dish with plastic wrap, place it in the refrigerator and allow it to marinate overnight.

3 When you are ready to cook the chicken, preheat the oven to 400 degrees. Remove the baking pan from the refrigerator, take off the plastic wrap and bake for 25–30 minutes until the chicken is cooked throughout.

Eating with your Hand

In India, it is polite to use your right hand for eating. Eating with the left hand is considered unclean and rude. Much attention is devoted to cleanliness, particularly for cooking and dining. In most Indian households, the individual preparing the meal bathes and puts on clean clothes before entering the kitchen. Produce and herbs are washed and dried outdoors, to prevent dirt from contaminating the immaculate cooking area.

About Chutney

Chutney is a tangy sweet condiment that is served with curry to balance its hot and pungent flavor. Look for chutney in the condiments section of your supermarket.

About Curry

Curry is not just one spice, but a blend of many Indian spices, ground together. Spices traditionally used in curry powder include coriander, ginger and turmeric, which gives the curry its bright yellow color. In India, chefs buy these spices whole and grind them into their own unique curry.

Shrimp Curry

INGREDIENTS *(serves 4)*

3 tablespoons salted butter
1 tablespoon flour
2 tablespoons curry powder
1/2 teaspoon salt
1 container (15 ounces) coconut milk
1 pound large shrimp (Ask the fish merchant to
    take off the shells and tails for you.)
1 small jar mango chutney

DIRECTIONS

1 Prepare the curry sauce. Melt 2 tablespoons of the butter in a small saucepan over low heat. Stir in the flour, salt, and curry with a wire whisk. Slowly add the coconut milk, a little a time, stirring constantly. Whisk for an additional 3–5 minutes, until the sauce is thickened. Stir in 2 tablespoons of the chutney, then remove from heat.

2 Cook the shrimp. Melt the remaining tablespoon of butter in a large skillet over medium heat. Add the shrimp and sauté until they turn pink and opaque, about 5 minutes.

3 Pour the warm curry sauce over the shrimp, stirring until the shrimp are well coated. Cover the pan and cook an additional 3 minutes over very low heat. Serve the curry over individual bowls of couscous (see recipe on page 46) or Basmati rice (see page 46).

4 Place the chutney in a serving dish and allow the guests to garnish their curry to taste.

Mango Pudding

INGREDIENTS *(serves 4)*

2 tablespoons mango nectar or orange juice
1 envelope plain (unflavored) gelatin
1/4 cup boiling water
3 ripe mangoes, peeled and cut into chunks
1 cup superfine sugar
juice of 1 lemon
1/2 pint heavy whipping cream

DIRECTIONS

1 Sprinkle the gelatin into a small bowl containing mango nectar or orange juice. Add the boiling water, stirring until the gelatin is dissolved. Set aside.

2 Puree the mangoes, sugar and lemon juice together in a blender or food processor until smooth.

3 Pour the mango mixture into a medium saucepan and bring to a boil over medium heat, stirring constantly. Lower heat and simmer an additional 15 minutes, stirring often. Remove from heat. Blend in the gelatin mixture. Cover with a plastic wrap and chill in the refrigerator for 40 minutes.

4 Whip the cream with an electric beater or mixer until it is stiff. Fold half of the whipped cream into the cooled mango mixture. Cover the remaining whipped cream with plastic wrap and refrigerate for later use.

5 Pour the mango mixture into 4 individual dessert cups. Refrigerate at least several hours before serving.

6 Just before serving, place a spoonful of whipped cream on top of each pudding.

Mango, King of Fruits

India is zealous in its love of mangoes. Regarded as the "king of fruits," mangoes are utilized in every aspect of Indian cuisine, from sweet to savory. Mangoes may be used in beverages, salads, chutney and desserts such as the Mango Pudding recipe here. Mango connoisseurs agree that the most succulent mango is the Alphonso variety, which is cultivated exclusively in Southern India.

ISRAEL

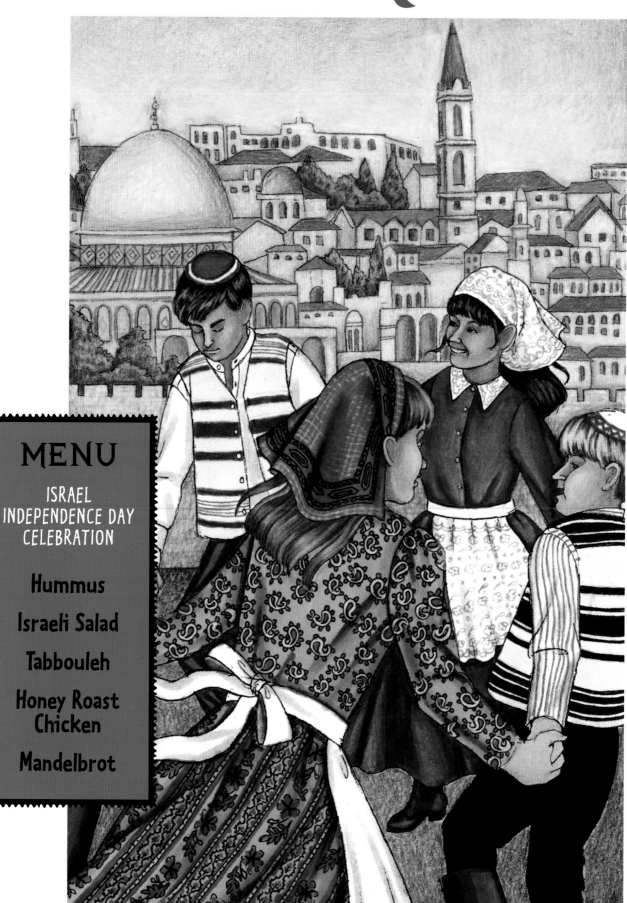

MENU

ISRAEL
INDEPENDENCE DAY
CELEBRATION

Hummus

Israeli Salad

Tabbouleh

Honey Roast
Chicken

Mandelbrot

Hummus

INGREDIENTS *(serves 4-6)*

1 can (15 ounces) chickpeas, drained
1/2 cup tahini (sesame paste)
juice of 2 lemons
2 garlic cloves, peeled and minced
1 teaspoon salt
carrot and celery sticks
pita bread, cut into wedges

DIRECTIONS

1 Combine the chickpeas, tahini, lemon juice, garlic and salt in a food processor or blender and puree until the mixture becomes a smooth paste. Place in a serving bowl and chill for several hours.

2 Serve with carrot and celery sticks, and pita wedges.

The Versatile Chickpea

Chickpeas are a quintessential element of Israeli cuisine. Chickpeas have a high protein content, making them an ideal addition to the Israeli diet, which is predominantly vegetarian. This legume is a primary ingredient in typical dishes such as Hummus and Falafel. At lunchtime in Israel, Hummus and Falafel stands enjoy a popularity similar to that of the hot dog carts found in the United States.

Yom Ha'atzma'uth

Each year, Israeli citizens celebrate *Yom Ha'atzma'uth* to mark the anniversary of their nation's independence, proclaimed on May 7, 1948. This festive day is celebrated with parades, festivals and fireworks. The children in the illustration on the facing page are performing a circular folk dance known as the hora. Originally created in Romania, the hora has been adopted as the national dance of Israel. The girls' festive blue-and-white folk costumes represent the national colors of Israel.

Eat Your Vegetables... for Breakfast?

Vegetables are an important of the Israeli diet since they are pareve or neutral, being made from neither dairy products nor meat. This means that Jews observing the dietary laws of Kashrut can enjoy them with either meat or dairy dishes. Salads, such as the Israeli Salad recipe featured on this page, are eaten at all meals, including breakfast. A typical Israeli breakfast is a healthy repast consisting of yogurt, cheeses and an array of fresh salads and vegetables.

Israeli Salad

INGREDIENTS *(serves 4)*

juice of 2 lemons
1/4 cup extra virgin olive oil
1 garlic clove, minced
1/2 teaspoon salt
1/4 teaspoon freshly ground pepper
2 large tomatoes, seeded and finely diced
2 cucumbers, peeled, seeded and finely diced
4 scallions, finely chopped, including the green part
1/2 cup chopped fresh parsley
2 tablespoons fresh chopped mint or dill

DIRECTIONS

1 Prepare dressing. Combine the lemon juice, olive oil, minced garlic, salt and pepper in a small bowl. Set aside.

2 Toss the salad. Combine the tomatoes, cucumbers, scallions, parsley and mint or dill. Pour the dressing over all the ingredients, stirring until salad is evenly coated.

Making the Desert Bloom

Israeli botanists have coaxed the dry desert soil of Israel into "blooming" through the creation of elaborate irrigation systems. Over the decades, Israel has cultivated enough produce to feed the entire nation, and has been able to export their fine produce as well. Israelis continue to pursue agricultural advances by adapting exotic fruits such as mangoes to their harsh climate, and by engineering new species such as seedless watermelon and the thornless prickly pear.

Tabbouleh

INGREDIENTS *(serves 4)*

3/4 cup bulgur wheat
3/4 cup boiling water
juice of 2 lemons
1/4 cup extra virgin olive oil
1/2 teaspoon salt
freshly ground pepper, to taste
1 large tomato, seeded and finely diced
1 cucumber, peeled, seeded and finely diced
1 red bell pepper, seeded and finely diced
1/4 cup finely chopped scallion, including the green part
1/2 cup fresh chopped parsley
1/2 cup fresh chopped mint

DIRECTIONS

1 Place the bulgur wheat in a bowl and add the boiling water. Cover with plastic wrap and allow the bulgur to soak until all the water is absorbed, approximately 30–40 minutes.

2 Prepare dressing. Combine the lemon juice, olive oil, salt and pepper in a small bowl. Set aside.

3 Add the tomatoes, cucumber, red bell pepper, scallion, parsley and mint to the soaked bulgur. Stir gently to combine.

4 Toss the salad. Pour the dressing over the bulgur mixture, stirring until all ingredients are evenly coated.

Moroccan Tabbouleh

To add a Moroccan twist to the recipe above, substitute 3/4 cup fresh couscous in place of the bulgur wheat and 1/2 cup fresh chopped coriander in place of the mint. Soak the couscous following the same directions as for the bulgur.

Israeli Cuisine

Israeli cuisine is a blend of many regional culinary influences. Jews emigrating from Eastern European countries such as Russia and Poland brought ancestral recipes to Israel. These Old World specialties included kugels, blintzes and soup dumplings. Moroccan contributions include couscous, dates and coriander. Bordering Mediterranean regions have also had an undeniable impact on the Israeli palate, as evidenced by the Israeli love of pita, Hummus, Falafel and phyllo pastries.

The Land of Milk and Honey

Honey has been symbolic of a sweet good life since biblical times when the promised land of Israel was described as the land of milk and honey. During Rosh Hashanah, the Jewish New Year, apples dipped in honey are eaten in celebration of a sweet new year. Cultures around the globe engage in similar symbolic rituals. In India, Muslims observe Ramadan by fasting during the daylight hours and enjoying sweet delicacies at night.

Honey Roast Chicken

INGREDIENTS *(serves 4)*

1/2 cup honey
1/4 cup frozen orange-juice concentrate, thawed
1/4 teaspoon ground ginger
1/2 teaspoon paprika
1/2 teaspoon salt
4 whole chicken breasts, skin removed (or one small
    chicken, quartered, skin removed)
1 orange, thinly sliced (do not peel)

DIRECTIONS

1 The day before you plan to serve the dish, prepare the honey sauce. Combine honey, orange-juice concentrate, ginger, paprika and salt in a small bowl. Place the chicken in a glass baking dish. Pour the sauce over the chicken, turning the chicken to ensure that each piece is evenly coated. Cover with plastic wrap and marinate in the refrigerator overnight.

2 When you are ready to bake the chicken, preheat the oven to 350 degrees. Remove the plastic wrap from the chicken. Place an orange slice on top of each piece of chicken. Bake, uncovered, for 50–55 minutes, basting occasionally with the honey sauce that settles to the bottom of the pan. The orange slices will become glazed during the baking process.

3 Remove the chicken from the baking pan and arrange on a serving platter. Pour the remaining sauce over the chicken.

Mandelbrot

INGREDIENTS *(makes about 24 biscuits)*

1/2 cup vegetable oil
1 cup superfine sugar
3 large eggs
2 teaspoons almond extract
1 teaspoon vanilla
1/4 teaspoon salt
2 teaspoons baking powder
2 1/4 cups sifted white flour
1 cup sliced almonds
1/2 cup chocolate chips

DIRECTIONS

1 Preheat oven to 350 degrees.

2 In a large bowl, combine the oil and sugar with a spoon. Add the eggs one at a time, beating well after each egg is added. Blend in the almond and vanilla extracts, salt, baking powder and flour. Mix until just combined. Gently fold in the almond and chocolate chips.

3 Divide the dough into two parts. Shape each half into a long wide log. Place logs on a greased baking sheet. Flatten slightly. Bake for 30 minutes.

4 Remove baked *Mandelbrot* from the baking sheet. Cool on a wire rack.

5 Preheat oven to 400 degrees. Cut the cooled *Mandelbrot* into 1/2-inch slices. Lie the slices of *Mandelbrot* on a greased baking sheet. Bake for about 10–12 minutes, until crisp and golden brown.

The Twice-Baked Cookie

Mandelbrot originated in Eastern Europe. In Hebrew, *Mandelbrot* means almond bread. The double-baking process allows these biscuits to store well, making them the perfect treat to serve on the Sabbath, when observant Jews do not bake. A similar twice-baked cookie is served in Italy. The Italians call their cookie *biscotti*, which translated literally means "twice-baked." Italians like to dip this hard crunchy biscuit into coffee or wine.

ITALY

MENU

SUNDAY
AFTERNOON DINNER

Antipasto

Garlic Bread

Pasta with
Homemade
Tomato Sauce

Veal Marsala

Tiramisu

Antipasto

INGREDIENTS *(serves 4)*

1/2 head iceberg lettuce
2 tomatoes, cut into wedges
1/4 pound each (sliced): Provolone cheese, Genoa salami,
    pepperoni and cappy ham
6–12 black olives
1 jar (7 ounces) marinated artichoke hearts, drained and
    quartered
1 jar (7 ounces) roasted red peppers, drained
1/4 cup olive oil
2 tablespoons balsamic vinegar
1 teaspoon each of sugar and dried oregano
salt and freshly ground pepper to taste

DIRECTIONS

1 Arrange lettuce in a thin layer on a medium-sized platter.
Decoratively arrange cheese, salami, pepperoni, olives and
artichoke hearts on top of the lettuce.

2 Prepare dressing. Combine oil, vinegar, sugar and oregano
in a small bowl. Mix with a wire whisk until well blended. Add
salt and pepper to taste. Pour dressing over the antipasto.

Italian Dining, Family-Style

The very heart of Italian cooking and dining centers around the family. In many regions of Italy, entire communities shut down for several hours during midday so that families can enjoy a meal together at home. In regions where modern life makes this custom impossible on a daily basis, Sunday dinner is still shared by the entire family. Family bonds are strengthened through lively conversation and the hearty enjoyment of lovingly prepared food.

About Freshly Ground Pepper

Whole black peppercorns, when freshly ground, have significantly more aroma and taste than the pre-ground black pepper we often buy. Freshly ground pepper adds an irresistible fragrance to every aspect of the Italian meal, from antipasto to meat. To grind pepper, simply place whole black peppercorns in a pepper mill and twist the mill while holding it over the food you wish to pepper. There are pepper mills to fit every budget, from inexpensive plastic models to expensive wooden designs.

Italian Breads

The unifying element in all Italian meals from breakfast to dinner is freshly baked bread. Breads vary from thin delicate bread sticks called *grissini* to hearty pizza-like focaccia, which is topped with fresh herbs. The fruit-filled *panettone* is a sweet bread traditionally served on Christmas morning. Many Italian breads are made with semolina, the heart of the wheat berry. Its yellow color gives the bread its characteristic golden cast. If there is an Italian bakery near you, sample a variety of these delicious breads.

Garlic Bread

INGREDIENTS *(serves 4-6)*

1 long loaf Italian bread
4-6 garlic cloves, finely chopped
4 tablespoons lightly salted butter, softened

DIRECTIONS

1 Preheat oven to 400 degrees. Cover a large baking pan with foil. Cut the bread in half lengthwise and place on the foil-covered pan, with the cut surface facing up.

2 Using a spoon, blend the garlic and butter in a small bowl. Spread the mixture evenly on the bread halves.

3 Bake for 20–25 minutes.

Bruschetta

INGREDIENTS *(serves 4-6)*

1 loaf Italian bread
2 garlic cloves, peeled and cut in half
2 tablespoons extra virgin olive oil
2 tomatoes, seeded and finely chopped
1 tablespoon chopped fresh basil
salt and pepper to taste

DIRECTIONS

1 Cut the bread into 1/2-inch slices. Lightly toast the bread.

2 Rub each slice of toast with the cut surface of a garlic clove. Drizzle with a small amount of olive oil. Top with chopped tomatoes and basil. Sprinkle with salt and pepper to taste.

Homemade Tomato Sauce

INGREDIENTS *(serves 4–6)*

1 tablespoon extra virgin olive oil
1 large onion, chopped
4 garlic cloves
2 tablespoons superfine sugar
1 teaspoon salt
1/4 teaspoon freshly ground black pepper
1 can (28 ounces) crushed tomatoes in puree
2 cans (4 ounces each) Italian-style tomato paste
1 teaspoon dried oregano
1 teaspoon dried Italian seasoning
8 fresh basil leaves, coarsely chopped (1 teaspoon dried
    basil may be substituted)
grated Parmesan or Romano cheese, to taste

DIRECTIONS

1 Heat the oil in a large saucepan over medium heat. Add the onion, cooking until translucent, about 10 minutes.

2 Add the garlic and sauté an additional 5 minutes. Sprinkle with the salt, sugar and black pepper, stirring to combine.

3 Add the crushed tomatoes, tomato paste, oregano, Italian seasoning and chopped basil. Cover and simmer for 2 hours, stirring occasionally. Taste the sauce and, if desired, add additional salt and freshly ground pepper.

4 To serve, ladle sauce over your favorite cooked pasta, such as spaghetti or penne. Top with grated Parmesan or Romano cheese and a sprinkling of freshly ground pepper.

Cuisines of Italy

The tomato sauce recipe given here is typical of Southern Italian cuisine, which is fresh and light. It is based on fresh produce such as tomatoes, garlic and basil, which flourish in the hot climate of Southern Italy. Olive oil, produced from regional olive trees, is used instead of butter. In contrast, Northern Italian cuisine is far richer. It includes meat and dairy products such as butter, cheese and cream. This rich diet utilizes the abundant cattle that are raised on the grassy hillsides of the north.

The Courses of an Italian Meal

An Italian dinner consists of numerous courses. The meal begins with assorted appetizers known as Antipasto, which literally translates as "before the meal." Soup or pasta arrives at the table next, followed by a meat or fish dish. Bread and wine are served during the meal to refresh the diner's palate after each course. Dessert can be as simple as fruit or as rich as Tiramisu. It is easy to understand why Italians spend two hours leisurely savoring their meals.

Veal Marsala

INGREDIENTS *(serves 4)*

1/4 cup flour
1/2 teaspoon salt
1/4 teaspoon freshly ground pepper
4 thin veal cutlets (about 1 pound total weight)
3 tablespoons olive oil
1/2 cup dry Marsala wine
2 tablespoons fresh lemon juice
1/2 cup beef broth
1 tablespoon flour

DIRECTIONS

1 Combine the flour, salt and pepper in a medium-sized bowl or dish. Dip each veal cutlet into the flour mixture, turning to coat both sides. Shake off any excess flour.

2 Heat the oil in a large skillet over medium-high heat. Add the floured veal cutlets, a few at a time. Cook for 2–3 minutes on each side, until veal is lightly brown. Remove the veal from the skillet, transfer to a warm plate and cover with foil to keep it warm while you are cooking the remaining cutlets.

3 Prepare Marsala sauce. Add the Marsala wine, lemon juice and beef broth to the drippings remaining in the skillet. Bring to a boil over medium-high heat, scraping the bottom of the skillet with a spoon to loosen any browned particles. Stir in the flour. Cook an additional 5 minutes, stirring constantly until sauce is thick.

4 Reduce heat to low and return the veal to the skillet. Cook an additional 3–5 minutes, or until cutlets are heated through. Place veal on a serving platter, pour the remaining sauce over the veal and serve.

Tiramisu

INGREDIENTS *(serves 4-6)*

1 packet unflavored gelatin
1 teaspoon sweet liqueur, such as Amaretto
6 egg yolks
1 cup superfine sugar
1 tablespoon cornstarch
2 containers (8 ounces each) Mascarpone cheese
2 teaspoons vanilla
1 pint heavy whipping cream
1 cup strong coffee or espresso, cooled
2 packages baked ladyfingers

DIRECTIONS

1 In a small bowl, combine gelatin and liqueur. Add 1/2 cup boiling water, stirring until all gelatin is dissolved. Set aside to cool.

2 Prepare Mascarpone mixture. In a metal bowl, beat the egg yolks, sugar and cornstarch together with a wire whisk. Set bowl in a pan of hot water and simmer for 15 minutes, whisking egg mixture constantly. Remove from heat. Beat in the Mascarpone cheese, vanilla and cooled gelatin mixture. Refrigerate.

3 Whip the heavy cream until stiff and gently fold into the cooled Mascarpone mixture.

4 Lightly dip ladyfingers in coffee and place them in a single layer in a serving bowl. Spoon half of the Mascarpone mixture on top. Place another layer of coffee-dipped ladyfingers on top. Finish with the second half of the Mascarpone mixture. If desired, garnish with ground cinnamon or chocolate shavings.

About Tiramisu

Tiramisu means "pick me up" in Italian. The caffeinated coffee used in this traditional dessert accounts for its energizing reputation. However, if you are sensitive to caffeine, you may substitute decaffeinated coffee. The Tiramisu will be equally delicious.

Chocolate Tiramisu

Add 1/2 cup unsweetened cocoa to the Mascarpone mixture. Top the finished dessert with fresh whipped cream.

JAPAN

MENU

SPRINGTIME MEAL AT MOUNT FUJI

Japanese Salad

Miso Soup

Beef Negimaki

Chicken Yakitori

Green Tea
Ice Cream

Japanese Salad

INGREDIENTS *(serves 4)*

1/2 pound daikon (Japanese white radish)
1 small carrot
1 teaspoon salt
1/4 cup rice vinegar
2 tablespoons sugar
1 teaspoon freshly grated ginger
1/4 cup dashi (If you cannot find dashi, a Japanese fish
  broth, you may substitute 2 tablespoons of soy sauce.)

DIRECTIONS

1 Peel the daikon and the carrot. Cut into short thin strips. Sprinkle the strips with the salt and knead it in. Set aside.

2 Combine the rice vinegar, sugar, ginger and dashi or soy sauce in a small pan. Bring to a boil. Set aside.

3 Rinse the salted daikon and carrot under cool running water. Drain the strips, squeezing out any remaining water.

4 Place the strips in a bowl and add the sweet vinegar dressing, stirring to combine. Cover with plastic wrap and refrigerate for at least 30 minutes.

5 Allow the salad to reach room temperature. Serve in small individual bowls.

Japanese Table Settings

While many Western cultures place one large serving bowl in the center of the table for the entire family, the Japanese prefer to use many tiny individual dishes. These delicate dishes are usually lacquered or ceramic, and designed by Japanese artisans.

Dining in Japan

The family depicted in the illustration on the facing page is dining in the traditional Japanese manner. They are kneeling on the tatami mat, having customarily left their shoes outside of the entrance to the room. The meal, designed to please the eye as well as the palate, is served on a low dining table. The parents pour sake into tiny cups for each other, as an expression of honor and respect. The rice-paper paneled shoji screen is pushed aside to reveal Mount Fuji, the sacred symbol of Japan.

Create Your Own Signature Miso

In Japan, each chef makes his or her own unique Miso Soup. There are many varieties of miso paste, ranging from white, which has a mild sweet flavor, to red, which has a strong pungent taste. Most Japanese chefs use dashi instead of water in their Miso Soup. Vegetables, such as snow pea pods, shiitake mushrooms and seaweed may be added, depending on the season. In the coastal areas of Japan, seafood, such as tiny clams, are often added to make Miso Soup unique. Varieties of miso paste, dashi and seaweed can be found at Japanese grocery stores. Experiment!

Miso Soup

INGREDIENTS (serves 4)

4 cups water
4 tablespoons red miso paste (You can buy miso paste at a Japanese grocery store or a health-food store.)
2 tablespoons soy sauce
2 tablespoons rice wine vinegar
2 tablespoons sherry or sake
1/4 pound firm tofu, cut into small cubes
6 scallions, thinly sliced, including the green part

DIRECTIONS

1 Bring the water to a boil in a medium-sized soup pot.

2 Add the miso paste to the boiling water and stir until dissolved. Reduce heat to a simmer and stir in the soy sauce, rice wine vinegar, sherry, tofu and scallions. Simmer for 2–3 minutes. Serve immediately.

The Honorable Soybean

Since ancient times, the Japanese diet has included a variety of foods made from the soybean. Tofu (soybean curd) and miso (soybean paste) were originally prepared and eaten by Buddhist priests whose strict vows forbade the consumption of meat. The first tofu shops available to the public were located within the Buddhist temples. These nutritious, protein-rich soy foods quickly became popular with the Japanese population at large. In Japan, Miso Soup is eaten at almost every meal, including breakfast.

Beef Negimaki

INGREDIENTS *(serves 4)*

1/2 cup dark soy sauce
1/4 cup sake (Japanese rice wine)
1/4 cup *mirin* (Japanese sweet cooking wine)
1/4 cup sugar
1/2 pound sirloin steak, thinly sliced
    (about 2–3 slices, 1/8- to 1/4-inch thick)
6 scallions, trimmed to fit the length of the steak
1 tablespoon sesame oil

DIRECTIONS

1 Prepare sauce. Combine soy sauce, sake, *mirin* and sugar in a small saucepan. Cook over medium heat until sauce is thick and syrupy, about 10–15 minutes. Pour the thickened sauce into a small bowl and set aside to cool.

2 Prepare beef rolls. Place a steak slice flat on a cutting board or other work surface and arrange two scallions along its edge. Roll the steak tightly around the scallions, until the steak is a cylinder. Tie each end of the cylinder with kitchen string to prevent it from unrolling. Repeat this process with the other steak slices.

3 Cook the beef rolls. Heat the sesame oil in a skillet over medium heat. Add the beef rolls and cook until they are brown on all sides, about 5 minutes. Pour the sauce over the rolls and bring it to a boil. Reduce heat and simmer 5 minutes. Remove the rolls from the skillet, cut off the string, and slice the rolls into 1-inch pieces. Spoon sauce over the sliced rolls.

Pampered Beef

In Japan, Buddhist law prohibited the consumption of beef for many centuries. During the Meji period in the late 1800s, beef was at last permitted in the Japanese diet, and dishes such as sukiyaki and *negimaki* became classics. Japan produces some of the finest beef in the world, despite a shortage of pasture. Although cattle raised in the Kobe region cannot graze, they enjoy unusual bovine luxuries, such as beer and daily massages, which contribute to the taste and tenderness of the beef.

Seasonal Cuisine

The seasons are the inspiration for Japanese cuisine. The gourmet awaits the delicacies unique to each season. In the spring, cherry-blossom tea is sipped as an accompaniment to cherry-blossom-pink cakes. The summer specialty is eel, which is consumed to give one strength to bear the hot and humid summer. Autumn brings the extravagant *matsutake* mushroom. During winter, the brave consume blowfish sushi, a delicacy that is fatal if not prepared correctly. The less adventurous curl up with *o-nabe*, a one-pot stew of chicken, meat or seafood and vegetables in broth, cooked at the table—the ultimate warming winter comfort food.

Chicken Yakitori

INGREDIENTS *(serves 4)*

1/2 cup teriyaki sauce
1/4 cup *mirin* (sweet Japanese cooking wine)
3 tablespoons sugar
1 teaspoon finely grated fresh ginger
4 boneless, skinless chicken breasts
2 small leeks

DIRECTIONS

1 Prepare marinade. Combine the teriyaki sauce, *mirin*, sugar and ginger together in a small saucepan. Cook over medium heat until marinade becomes thick and syrupy, about 15 minutes. Set aside to cool.

2 When you are ready to cook the chicken, preheat the broiler. Wash the leeks and cut them into small pieces, about 1 inch in size. Thread the chicken and the leeks on a long metal skewer, alternating pieces of chicken and pieces of leek. This recipe will make enough to fill 4 long skewers.

3 Place the skewered chicken and leeks in a broiling pan. Brush with the marinade. Broil the skewers for 5 minutes. Serve the skewers over a bed of white rice.

Harmony with Nature

Traditional Japanese clothing is inspired by the seasons of nature. The woman in the illustration on page 62 is wearing a kimono decorated with cherry blossoms and butterflies to commemorate spring. A pink and white kimono called a *hanagoromo* is worn exclusively for cherry-blossom viewing.

Green Tea Ice Cream

NOTE: This recipe requires an ice-cream maker.

INGREDIENTS *(serves 8)*

2 cups whipping cream
2 cups half and half
1 cup superfine sugar
1/4 cup *matcha* (You can find this powdered green tea
in a Japanese grocery store.)

DIRECTIONS

1 Mix the whipping cream, half and half, sugar and *matcha* together. Stir until the sugar is dissolved and all ingredients are well blended.

2 Place the mixture in your ice-cream maker and follow the processing instructions supplied by the manufacturer of the ice-cream maker.

The History of Tea in Japan

Green tea was first sipped in Japan during the eighth century by Zen Buddhist monks in order to keep awake during all-night prayer vigils. The tea ceremony that evolved is based on Zen philosophy. Eventually, the consumption of tea and the accompanying ritual spread to the general Japanese population.

Japanese green tea (*matcha*) is made from the same plant used to produce black tea in China, but the processing is different. Tea leaves retain their green color if they are steamed immediately after picking, thus preventing the leaves from oxidizing and darkening. The green leaves are then dried and ground into a fine powder for *matcha*.

The Japanese Tea Ceremony

For this ceremony, tea is prepared individually for each guest. The host spoons *matcha* into a tea cup, then skillfully beats in hot water using a bamboo whisk. Kneeling, the host bows, presenting the frothy tea to an honored guest. The guest bows, sips the tea, admiring its taste and texture, while taking pleasure in the decorative cups and utensils. The focus of the tea ceremony is harmony, tranquility and contemplation. One must study for years to fully master *Chado*, the Way of Tea.

MEXICO

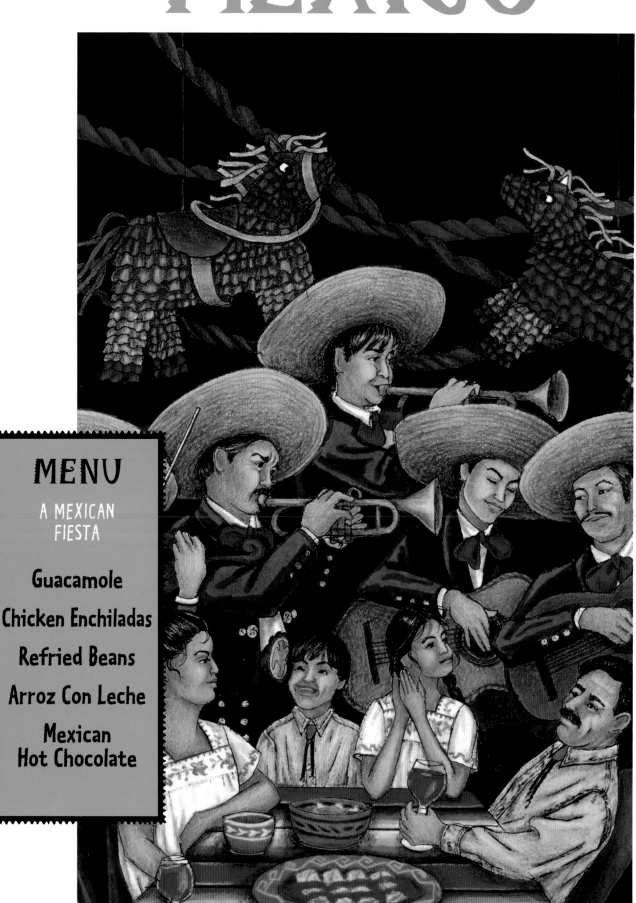

MENU

A MEXICAN
FIESTA

Guacamole

Chicken Enchiladas

Refried Beans

Arroz Con Leche

Mexican
Hot Chocolate

Guacamole

INGREDIENTS *(serves 4)*

1 small Spanish onion, finely chopped
juice of 2 limes
1/2 teaspoon salt
1/4 teaspoon black pepper
2 ripe Hass avocados
1 ripe tomato, seeds removed, finely chopped
2 tablespoons chopped fresh cilantro
1 jalapeno pepper, seeds removed, finely chopped
1 bag tortilla chips

DIRECTIONS

1 Using a fork, mash the onion, cilantro, jalapeno pepper, salt and pepper together in a medium-sized bowl. Mashing will release the flavor of the cilantro, onion and jalapeno pepper. The mixture should remain coarse and chunky. Stir in lime juice.

2 Cut the avocados lengthwise completely around. Pry the avocados in half and remove the pits. Using a spoon, scoop out all the soft green flesh from inside each avocado half and place in the bowl containing the onion/cilantro mixture. Mash together, using a fork, until it is fairly smooth. Gently stir in the chopped tomato. Serve immediately with the tortilla chips.

About Hass Avocados

Hass avocados are the black and bumpy variety imported to the United States from Mexico. Their creamy flavorful flesh is far superior to the smooth green avocados from Florida. Whenever possible, buy Hass avocados for your Guacamole.

Mexican Fiestas

The family illustrated on the facing page is enjoying a fiesta: a Mexican celebration. They are being serenaded by strolling musicians called mariachi. Wearing traditional costumes, the mariachi perform lively melodies and soulful ballads. The highlight of the fiesta is the pinata, the colorful animal featured at the top of the drawing. The papier-mâché pinata, filled with candy and small toys, is hung from the ceiling. Children make a game of hitting it with a stick until it breaks, spilling candy and toys for all to share.

Nachos: A Great Way to Use Leftover Jack Cheese and Refried Beans

INGREDIENTS

tortilla chips
Refried Beans
Monterey Jack cheese

DIRECTIONS

1 Preheat oven to 350 degrees.

2 Gently spread about one tablespoon of Refried Beans on each tortilla chip. Place the filled tortilla chips on a greased cookie sheet.

3 Top each tortilla chip with one tablespoon of shredded Monterey Jack cheese

4 Bake for 10–12 minutes, until cheese is melted.

Refried Beans

INGREDIENTS *(serves 4)*

1 cup dried pinto beans (You may substitute a
    16-ounce can of pinto or kidney beans, drained,
    and begin the recipe with step 3.)
2 tablespoons vegetable oil
1 onion, finely chopped
1 garlic clove, minced
1/2 cup shredded Monterey Jack cheese

DIRECTIONS

1 The day before you plan to serve this dish, rinse and sort through beans, removing any irregular ones. Place the rinsed beans in a bowl and add 3 cups water. Discard any beans that float to the top. Soak the beans overnight.

2 Drain the beans and place them in a saucepan. Cover with fresh cold water and simmer, covered, over low heat until beans are tender, about one hour. Set aside, undrained.

3 Heat the oil in a large skillet. Add the onion and sauté until golden brown, about 10–15 minutes. Add the garlic and sauté an additional 5 minutes.

4 Reduce heat to low and add the beans to the sautéed onion and garlic. Mash the mixture with a fork or potato masher, until the beans are coarsely pureed. Remove from heat.

5 Garnish the beans with a sprinkling of shredded Monterey Jack cheese. Serve as a side dish with enchiladas.

Cooking Lite

This recipe, adapted to lighter taste, uses oil in the place of the lard used in traditional Mexican refried-bean recipes.

Chicken Enchiladas

INGREDIENTS *(serves 4)*

2 tablespoons vegetable oil
4 boneless, skinless chicken breasts, cut into
    1/2-inch strips
1 onion, cut into 1/4-inch strips
8 corn tortillas
1 jar commercial enchilada sauce or homemade
    enchilada sauce (see recipe at right)
12 ounces Monterey Jack cheese, grated
1 container (8 ounces) sour cream

DIRECTIONS

1 Preheat the oven to 400 degrees.

2 Heat the oil in a large skillet. Add the chicken, cooking over medium heat 10–12 minutes, or until strips begin to brown. Add the onion and peppers, cooking an additional 5–7 minutes.

3 Place a portion of the chicken, onion and pepper mixture in the center of a tortilla. Fold and overlap right and left sides of tortilla. Place the filled tortilla in a baking pan, with the overlapping edges facing down. Repeat for all 8 tortillas.

4 Cover the filled tortillas with enchilada sauce. Sprinkle with the shredded Monterey Jack cheese and bake for 10–15 minutes, until the cheese is melted. Spoon one tablespoon of sour cream on each enchilada immediately before serving.

Homemade Enchilada Sauce

INGREDIENTS

1 tablespoon corn oil
1 onion, finely chopped
2 garlic cloves, minced
1 can (28 ounces) tomatoes in puree
2 tablespoons chili powder

DIRECTIONS

1 Heat the oil in a large skillet. Add the onion, cooking until soft, about 8–10 minutes. Add the garlic, cooking an additional 3 minutes.

2 Add the tomatoes and chili powder. Simmer, uncovered, for 30 minutes.

Beef or Seafood Enchiladas

One pound of sirloin steak, cut into 1/2-inch strips, or one pound shrimp may be substituted for the chicken. Follow the same directions.

Arroz Con Leche

INGREDIENTS *(serves 4)*

1 cup water
1 cinnamon stick
1/2 cup uncooked short-grain white rice
1 can (14 ounces) sweetened condensed milk
1 cup fresh whole milk
1 teaspoon vanilla extract
1/4 cup raisins
2 egg yolks
1 teaspoon ground cinnamon for garnish

DIRECTIONS

1 Bring water and cinnamon stick to a boil in a saucepan over medium heat, stirring occasionally. Add the rice and return to a boil. Cover, reduce heat and simmer 15–20 minutes, until liquid is absorbed.

2 Add the condensed milk and whole milk to the cooked rice in the saucepan. Simmer, uncovered, 15–20 minutes, until the mixture begins to thicken.

3 Remove from heat and discard cinnamon stick. Stir in vanilla and raisins and allow to cool for 5 minutes.

4 Blend the egg yolks into the warm rice mixture. Return the saucepan to low heat, cooking 3–5 additional minutes, until mixture thickens. Transfer to a serving bowl and refrigerate several hours. Sprinkle with cinnamon before serving.

Mexican Hot Chocolate

INGREDIENTS *(serves 4)*

3 cups whole milk

1 piece (3.3 ounces) Mexican chocolate (Mexican chocolate can be found in Hispanic grocery stores. If you cannot find Mexican chocolate, substitute equal amounts of sweet baking chocolate, and be sure to use a cinnamon garnish, as Mexican chocolate has a cinnamon flavor.)

whipped cream (optional, for garnish)

ground cinnamon (optional, for garnish)

whole cinnamon sticks (optional, for garnish)

Chocolate: Food of the Gods

Since ancient times, chocolate has been exalted to a sacred status in Mexico. The Aztecs were said to have used cocoa beans as a form of currency. Chocolate, originally unsweetened, was whipped into a brew fit for only the most pious of priests. The botanical name for chocolate, *theobroma*, literally means "food of the gods." Over time, the hot chocolate drink became sweetened. Its consumption spread to the rest of the Mexican population, where it is still held in high esteem.

DIRECTIONS

1 Combine the milk and Mexican chocolate in a saucepan. Simmer over low heat, stirring continuously, until the chocolate is melted. Immediately remove from heat.

2 Pour the hot chocolate into a blender and process until frothy.

3 Pour into mugs. If desired, top with whipped cream and sprinkle with ground cinnamon or simply garnish with a cinnamon stick.

The Molinillo

Although the recipe on this page directs you to place the hot chocolate in a blender, in Mexico it would be blended using a *molinillo*. A *molinillo* is a wooden tool specifically designed to whip chocolate into a froth.

SPAIN

MENU

ANDALUSIAN
FLAMENCO FESTIVAL

Sangria
Fruit Punch

Roasted
Pimientos

Gazpacho

Seafood Paella

Flan

Sangria Fruit Punch

INGREDIENTS *(serves 4)*

4 limes
2 lemons
2 oranges
1 can frozen fruit-juice concentrate (A red-colored juice
    such as cranberry juice will look the most traditional.)
1 can cold water
ice

DIRECTIONS

1 Squeeze two of the limes, one of the lemons and one of the oranges. Strain the juice through a fine strainer and pour into a large pitcher. Add the can of juice concentrate. Fill the empty juice can with cold water and pour into the pitcher. Stir well to combine.

2 Cut the remaining lemon, orange and two limes into thin slices. Add the slices to the juice in the pitcher. The fruit slices will float decoratively. Refrigerate for several hours before serving.

3 Add ice to the pitcher and stir prior to serving. Pour into festive glasses.

Traditional Sangria in Spain

In Spain, traditional sangria is made with red wine. If you wish to prepare traditional sangria for adults, substitute one cup of red wine in place of the can of water and add 1/4 cup of triple sec (orange liqueur).

The Gypsy Dance of Spain

Flamenco is a creation of the Andalusian gypsies. Originally, it involved only voice and guitar. Emphasis was placed on duende, the passion of the artist; the most passionate received shouts of "Ole!" Eventually, dance became part of the flamenco. With dresses swirling, dancers in thick-heeled shoes stamp out their rhythms to the cries of *"Viva la manquina escribir!"* meaning "Long live the typewriter!" Flamenco continues to thrive in the many summer festivals in Andalusia.

Tapas, the Little Bites of Spain

Spanish meal patterns are similar to those of other Mediterranean regions. Lunch is eaten close to 2 p.m., while dinner rarely begins before 9 p.m. Tapas are appetizers often eaten before dinner, although hearty servings of a variety of tapas can comprise an entire meal. Traditional selections found in the tapas bars of Spain include small bites of spicy chorizo sausage, fried shellfish and roasted pimientos. Spanish sherry is often sipped with tapas.

Roasted Pimientos

INGREDIENTS *(serves 4)*

4 whole red bell peppers, washed
2 tablespoons extra virgin olive oil
1 tablespoon sherry vinegar or balsamic vinegar
1 garlic clove, minced
salt and freshly ground black pepper, to taste

DIRECTIONS

1 Preheat oven to 500 degrees.

2 Cut the peppers in half and remove the cores, seeds and ribs. Slice the peppers into long strips. Place the peppers in a single layer, skin side up in the roasting pan. Add approximately 1/4-inch water to the pan. Roast the peppers, uncovered, for 20 minutes or until they begin to blacken.

3 Remove the peppers from the oven and immediately transfer them to a bowl. Cover the bowl with foil, and allow the peppers to cool for 30 minutes.

4 Peel the blackened skins off the peppers.

5 Prepare the dressing. In a small bowl, combine the olive oil, vinegar, garlic, salt and pepper with a wire whisk. Pour the dressing over the pepper strips and stir to combine. Cover and refrigerate several hours before serving.

Salad or Tapas

Roasted Pimientos may be served as a first-course salad or as a tapa (see sidebar).

Gazpacho

INGREDIENTS *(serves 4)*

4 large tomatoes, chopped, with seeds removed
1 medium cucumber, peeled, finely chopped,
    with seeds removed
1 small red pepper, finely diced, with core
    and seeds removed
1 sweet onion, finely chopped
2 garlic cloves, finely chopped
2 cups tomato juice
1 tablespoon olive oil
1 teaspoon salt
1 tablespoon sugar
1/4 cup fresh lime (about 2-3 limes)
2 tablespoons sherry vinegar or balsamic vinegar

DIRECTIONS

1 Combine all the prepared vegetables in a large bowl. Add the tomato juice, oil, salt and lime juice. Stir until well blended.

2 Pour half of the soup into a blender or food processor and puree. Pour the pureed soup back into the bowl with the remainder of the soup. Stir to combine. Cover and refrigerate at least several hours. Serve chilled.

Liquid Salad

Gazpacho has often been described as liquid salad. In Spain, regional Gazpachos vary, from smooth versions, which have been mashed into a silky paste with a mortar and pestle, to versions so chunky they resemble salads. The recipe above is smooth, with some diced vegetables reserved to add texture. If you find a smooth soup more appealing, puree all the soup instead of half, as the recipe indicates.

Gazpacho, the Refreshing Cold Soup of Spain

Gazpacho was created in Andalusia. The ingredients included bread slices and lots of olive oil, providing nourishment to those working the fields under the scorching Spanish sun. Gazpachos have since become lighter and generally do not include bread or large amounts of oil. While red Gazpacho is traditional in Andalusia, other regions of Spain are noted for their own variations, including green herbal Gazpachos and sweet white Gazpachos made with almonds.

Paella, the Spanish Skillet

Paella is the Spanish name for a heavy double-handled skillet. The paella skillet is used to prepare the saffroned rice and seafood dish that became known as paella. The original paella, created in Valencia, featured the addition of chicken to the seafood-based recipe at right. Regional variations may also include exotic shellfish such as mussels or squid. Slices of spicy chorizo sausage occasionally provide a zesty accent.

Seafood Paella

INGREDIENTS *(serves 4)*

1/4 cup olive oil
1 medium sweet onion, peeled and chopped
2 garlic cloves, finely chopped
1/2 pound each shrimp and scallops
1 can (16 ounces) crushed tomatoes
1 cup uncooked short-grain white rice
1 cup water
1/2 teaspoon salt
1/4 teaspoon ground red pepper
1/2 teaspoon saffron or ground turmeric
1 small jar (4 ounces) sliced pimientos, drained
1/2 cup frozen peas, thawed

DIRECTIONS

1 Heat the oil in a large skillet over a medium heat. Add the onion and garlic and cook until translucent, about 5 minutes. Add the shrimp and scallops; cook for 4–5 minutes, stirring constantly, until shrimp turns pink and scallops become opaque and firm.

2 Stir in the canned tomatoes, including the liquid. Add the rice, water, salt, red pepper and saffron or turmeric. Stir well, cover and reduce heat to low. Simmer, covered, for 20 minutes, until most of the liquid is absorbed.

3 Stir in the pimientos and peas and simmer 5 more minutes.

About Saffron

Saffron, the orange stigma of the crocus flower, is prized for the golden-orange color it lends to food. However, it is quite expensive. Turmeric is a less-expensive alternative, and also provides a fine golden color.

Flan

INGREDIENTS *(serves 4)*

1/2 cup brown sugar
3 eggs
1/3 cup superfine sugar
1 can evaporated milk
2 teaspoons vanilla extract
1/8 teaspoon salt

DIRECTIONS

1 Preheat the oven to 325 degrees.

2 Melt the brown sugar in a small saucepan over low heat until the sugar becomes syrupy. Divide the syrup among 4 custard cups. Rotate cups to be certain that the syrup evenly coats the bottom of each cup.

3 Mix eggs, superfine sugar, evaporated milk, vanilla and salt together with a wire whisk until well-blended. Pour the mixture equally into the 4 prepared custard cups.

4 Place cups in a baking pan with high sides. Carefully pour hot water into the baking pan, being careful not to allow any water inside the custard cups. The sides of the cups should be half covered with water. Bake for 40–45 minutes or until a knife inserted in the center comes out clean. Remove custard cups from the pan of water and refrigerate for several hours before serving.

5 To serve, place an individual serving plate on top of each custard dish. Invert plate and lift the custard dish. The brown sugar syrup that coated the bottom of the cups now makes a beautiful and delicious topping.

Flan, a Heavenly Dessert

In Spain, custard desserts have long been identified with convent nuns. Winemakers, using egg whites to clarify their wine, donated the egg yolks to local convents. The resourceful nuns used the yolk to create confections such as Flan, *tocinellos de cielo* and candied egg yolks. Villagers quickly discovered these unique sweets, turning them into a profitable industry for the nuns. Spanish nuns continue this tradition today, listing the creations available for purchase on the convent doors.

INDEX